I0152317

HEAVENLY ANGEL

LAY LAY

EXPLAINS WHY

CHILDREN AND

SPORTS ARE

DEFINITELY

A RELIGION IN

TODAY'S SOCIETY

PUBLISHING COMPANY

TABLE OF CONTENTS

CHILDREN AND SPORTS

MOSES

BIBLIOGRAPHY

ABOUT THE AUTHOR

I was dedicated to Jesus Christ of Nazareth as an infant and accepted Him as my Lord and Savior around seven years old when a visiting youth group led me in prayer at the alter. During my Salvation Prayer I asked Jesus to use me in a special ministry. Something that very few other Christians would want to do. I saw all the people just sitting in the pews, the ushers, and the Sunday School teachers and realized any Christian could do that. I wanted something different. One day in church service there was a visiting minister at a church I was visiting as well. The Minister said, "Jesus is going to make you a 'Healer of a Heart'". Then he asked me if I knew what that meant. I said, "No." the minister said, "I don't either, but whatever it is, Jesus is going to use you in a powerful way.

Helping Rachael, Jesus showed me what a 'Healer of the Heart' is. During the course of me helping Rachael to the 'Promised Land', a real Heavenly Angel named Lay Lay and I were allowed one hour one day to talk about Spiritual and Family situations from the King James Version of the Word of God. These books are designed to answer a lot of Spiritual Questions not even your minister can answer or your Church Denomination. I know theology Doctors who can't tell you how people other than Noah and his family made it past the 'Great Flood', yet their names are listed in the King James Version of the Word of God right after the 'World Wide Flood'. These books explain that and much more. I have written these books to tell the whole truth about the Word of God no matter how difficult it may be for me or others. Yes, there are things I write in these books that I don't even like, but in all fairness and total honestly, I must say the WHOLE TRUTH. The title of this book is 100% real. HEAVENLY ANGEL LAY LAY explained to me why gays, lesbians, bi-sexuals, and transsexuals DO NOT go to Heaven. I know this may make some people mad, but I won't 'Candy Coat' the Word of the Living God or what any Heavenly Angel said to me.

INTRODUCTION

The first section of this book talks about why children and sports are definitely a religion in today's society and how they became a religion in the first place. The second section of this book tells about Jacob and Joseph. All scriptures are taken from the King James Version of the Word of God. This book contains an excerpt from my book. MATTHEW'S WORD 'TWO':REAL WORD OF GOD BIBLE.

BOOKS WRITTEN BY WALTER BURCHETT, BA:

MATTHEW'S WORD 'TWO':REAL WORD OF GOD BIBLE   ISBN: 1-4116-6995-9

HEAVENLY ANGEL LAY LAY EXPLAINS WHY ADAM WAS NEVER CURSED
                                                                                  ISBN: 978-1-84728-176-0

HEAVENLY ANGEL LAY LAY EXPLAINS WHY ABORTED BABIES DO NOT GO TO HEAVEN
                                                                                  ISBN: 978-0-6151-7470-9

HEAVENLY ANGEL LAY LAY EXPLAINS THE BIBLICAL GROUNDS FOR MARRIAGE,
        SEPARATION, AND DIVORCE   ISBN: 978-0-6151-7481-5

HEAVENLY ANGEL LAY LAY EXPLAINS WHY PROFESSIONAL COUNSELORS HAVE 'HARDENED
        HEARTS'   ISBN: 978-0-6151-7482-2

HEAVENLY ANGEL LAY LAY EXPLAINS THE DIFFERENCE BETWEEN A 'COLD CHRISTIAN' AND
        A 'BACKSLIDER'   ISBN: 978-0-6151-7483-9

HEAVENLY ANGEL LAY LAY EXPLAINS WHICH BIBLE TO READ, WHICH BIBLE NOT TO READ,
        AND WHY   ISBN: 978-0-6151-7484-6

HEAVENLY ANGEL LAY LAY EXPLAINS WHY GAYS, LESBIANS, BI-SEXUALS, AND
        TRANSSEXUALS DO NOT GO TO HEAVEN   ISBN: 978-0-6151-7485-3

HEAVENLY ANGEL LAY LAY EXPLAINS WHY CHILDREN AND SPORTS ARE DEFINITELY A
        RELIGION IN TODAY'S SOCIETY   ISBN: 978-0-6151-7486-0

HEAVENLY ANGEL LAY LAY EXPLAINS WHAT 'MANY ARE CALLED, BUT FEW ARE CHOSEN
        REALLY MEANS   ISBN: 978-0-6151-7487-7

HEAVENLY ANGEL LAY LAY AND GUARDIAN ANGEL SHADOW GUESS THE REAL AGE OF THE
        EARTH   ISBN: 978-0-6151-7488-4

AN ABUSED MAN'S BATTLES, TRYING TO PROTECT HIS BOYS   ISBN: 978-0-6151-5191-5

HEAVENLY ANGEL LAY LAY

EXPLAINS WHY

CHILDREN AND SPORTS ARE DEFINITELY A RELIGION IN TODAY'S SOCIETY

(The following is an excerpt from my book MATTHEW'S WORD 'TWO':REAL WORD OF GOD BIBLE when Heavenly Angel Lay Lay and I had a chance to talk one hour one day during the year I was allowed to not only talk to, but work with three different Heavenly Angels)

CHILDREN AND SPORTS ARE DEFINITELY A RELIGION IN TODAY'S SOCIETY

I asked, "What about the scripture, about the way being narrow?" Lay Lay said, "In Matthew 7:13-14 (KJV) the Word of God says, 'Enter ye in at the strait gate: for wide is the gate, and broad is the way, that leadeth to destruction, and many there be which go in thereat; Because strait is the gate, and narrow is the way, which leadeth unto life, and few there be that find it.'

The first part is talking about destruction being easy.   Not accepting Jesus in the first place, due to 'false prophets', 'false doctrine', etc. The 'gate being narrow' is talking about the true doctrine and way; the Word of God and accepting Jesus as your Lord and Savior. 'Few there be that find it.' Using the Israelites as an example, Jesus is giving a comparison, between right way and the way of the world, the false doctrines, the Atheists, the Agnostics, the Druids, the Wicca's, the Satanists, all the other religions including the human's own children. *Children and sports are definitely a religion in your society today. In the United States the so called 'Religion' is Christianity because that's what your country was founded for, the freedom to worship the Father in Heaven, Jesus Christ of Nazareth, and the Holy Spirit without any governmental interference. In other words, the government can't tell you how to worship the Father in Heaven, Jesus Christ of Nazareth, and the Holy Spirit so long as you do worship them. Worshipping any other god or deity is actually going against the founding fathers and the Constitution of the United States of America.* If a parent puts their child above Jesus, then the child becomes the parent's religion. Men are noted for their religion as being in some kind of sports, they worship sports instead of Jesus, that's their religion, that's who or what they worship, it's another form of Idolism. Mother's putting their children first is Idolism. Human parents get so wrapped up in their children's lives and want to do what's best for the child; they actually push Jesus out of the way for their own children, like Mandy. Mandy was going against Jesus, Himself, holding Detta back from Crossing Over and worshipping Rachael, the vessel, her daughter, believing in her heart she was doing the right thing because she only wanted what's best for Rachael, the vessel, yet Mandy can't see Rachael's heart, Mandy can't see the future of Rachael burning in Hell for all eternity if Mandy keeps on holding Detta back. It's Jesus Christ of Nazareth first, then the parents, then the children. The children are to be under the father who is the head of the house and mother who is to 'desire' to do as her husband asks according to the Word of God, not above Jesus Christ of Nazareth. So many human parents have been brain washed from the media that children come first.   One big problem Christians have is once they get saved and learn in the scriptures about all these salvation passages, they start looking around in their own churches and families, looking for humans that scripture may fit. They don't take into account all the other different religions that claim to be Christians, or don't profess Christianity to begin with. The first thing they need to do is get Grounded in the Word of God first, then once that is done and their own family is straightened out they can go out and help others, but leave their church doctrine out of the witnessing. Just talk about how Jesus has changed their lives for the best so the ones who they are witnessing to will want to accept Jesus as their Lord and Savior. The church doctrine can come later, after the conversion if the converted human wants to know." I asked, "If the parents keep putting Jesus second or third, what will happen to them?" Lay Lay said, "They will burn in Hell. Those who do not put Jesus first in their lives forsaking all others, including their own children, are not worthy to enter into the Kingdom of Heaven. That 'narrow gate' was for the Israelites, it's for everyone now. The Israelites chose to go back to Idolism as a Nation. Now it's for everyone to aim for and it's the same narrow gate no matter if the human is an Atheist, Agnostic, Christian Science, any other man made church or religion, or a parent worshipping their own child. Christians already have a Master Key to open it. The Master Key is called, 'The Crucifixion, Blood, and Resurrection of Jesus

Christ of Nazareth and accepting Jesus Christ of Nazareth as their Lord and Savior with all their heart. It's just a few of the Israelites that will accept Jesus. If Christians would put as much effort into working on their own walk with Jesus as they do judging other Christian's walks with Jesus, there wouldn't be so many hard feelings in the churches today, attendance and worship services would skyrocket, no one likes to be judged yet, it's not judgment time yet. The dead in Christ haven't even been resurrected yet.

The only time a Christian can judge is when the Word of God has already judged and condemned that particular abomination, like the abominations committed in Sodom and the other cities, or the 'sons of God', or Satan being doomed forevermore. Then it's not really the Christian who is judging, it's the Father in Heaven who has already judged that abomination, Christians are just repeating what the Word of God already says. You could look at it like reading an 'Order of the Court' that has already been handed down and signed by the judge. Those particular offenses have already been judge upon."

MOSES
CONTINUED

(CONTINUED FROM: HEAVENLY ANGEL LAY LAY EXPLAINS WHY CHILDREN AND SPORTS ARE DEFINITELY A RELIGION IN TODAY'S SOCIETY)

MOSES

Exodus 3:1-22

1) Now Moses kept the flock of Jethro his father in law, the priest of Midian: and he (Moses) led the flock to the backside of the desert, and came to the mountain of God, even to Horeb.

2) And the angel of the LORD appeared unto him in a flame of fire out of the midst of a bush: and he (Moses) looked, and, behold, the bush burned with fire, and the bush was not consumed.

3) And Moses said, I will now turn aside, and see this great sight, why the bush is not burnt.

4) And when the LORD saw that he (Moses) turned aside to see, God called unto him out of the midst of the bush, and said, Moses, Moses. And he (Moses) said, Here am I.

5) And he (God) said, Draw not nigh hither (Do not come over here): put off thy (your) shoes from off thy (your) feet, for the place whereon thou standest is holy ground.

6) Moreover he (God) said, I am the God of thy father, the God of Abraham, the God of Isaac, and the God of Jacob. And Moses hid his face; for he was afraid to look upon God.

7) And the LORD said, I have surely seen the affliction of my people which are in Egypt, and have heard their cry by reason of their taskmasters; for I know their sorrows;

8) And I am come down (some people can't figure out why God has to move around to do things, when the Word of God says

God is going to come down, it means God is going to start using His Supernatural Power for a specific purpose according to His will. In this case, God is going to use His Supernatural Power to deliver the Israelites out of the land of Egypt) to deliver them (the Israelites) out of the hand of the Egyptians, and to bring them (the Israelites) up out of that land unto a good land and a large, unto a land flowing with milk and honey; unto the place of the Canaanites, and the Hittites, and the Amorites, and the Perizzites, and the Hivites, and the Jebusites.

9) Now therefore, behold, the cry of the children of Israel is come unto me: and I have also seen the oppression (this is a good example of what Heavenly Angel Lay Lay was talking about when she explained Demonic Oppression compared to Demonic Possession) wherewith the Egyptians oppress them (the children of Israel). (Remember, the Egyptians were 'idol worshippers', they worshipped Satan, Demonic Oppression and Demonic Possession)

10) Come now therefore, and I will send thee (you) unto Pharaoh, that thou mayest bring forth my people the children of Israel out of Egypt.

11) And Moses said unto God, Who am I, that I should go unto Pharaoh, and that I should bring forth the children of Israel out of Egypt?

12) And he (God) said, Certainly I will be with thee (you); and this shall be a token [something representing something else: something that represents, expresses, or is a symbol of something else. (Encarta ® World English Dictionary © & (P) 1998-2004 Microsoft Corporation. All rights reserved.)] unto thee (you), that I have sent thee (you): When thou hast (you have) brought forth the people out of Egypt, ye (you) shall serve God upon this mountain.

13) And Moses said unto God, Behold, when I come unto the children of Israel, and shall say unto them (the children of Israel), The God of your fathers hath sent me unto you; and they (the children of Israel) shall say to me, What is his name? what shall I say unto them?

14) And God said unto Moses, I AM THAT I AM: and he said,

Thus shalt thou (you) say unto the children of Israel, I AM hath sent me unto you.

15) And God said moreover unto Moses, Thus shalt thou say unto the children of Israel, the LORD God of your fathers, the God of Abraham, the God of Isaac, and the God of Jacob, hath sent me unto you: this is my name for ever, and this is my memorial unto all generations.

16) Go, and gather the elders of Israel together, and say unto them, The LORD God of your fathers, the God of Abraham, of Isaac, and of Jaccb, appeared unto me, saying, I have surely visited you, and seen that which is done to you in Egypt:

17) And I have said, I will bring you up out of the affliction of Egypt unto the land of the Canaanites, and the Hittites, and the Amorites, and the Perizzites, and the Hivites, and the Jebusites, unto a land flowing with milk and honey.

18) And they shall hearken (listen) to thy voice: and thou shalt come, thou and the elders of Israel, unto the king of Egypt, and ye (you) shall say unto him (the king of Egypt), The LORD God of the Hebrews hath met with us: and now let us go, we beseech thee (ask you), three days' journey into the wilderness, that we may sacrifice to the LORD our God.

19) And I am sure that the king of Egypt will not let you go, no, not by a mighty hand. (God is already telling Moses that the king of Egypt will refuse to let the children of Israel go)

20) And I will stretch out my hand, and smite (kill) Egypt with all my wonders (**all the Supernatural Force necessary to make the king of Egypt let the children of Israel go. Now for a personal note, with all the scientists out there who can explain this and explain that and still want proof that God exists, why is it so hard for you to think for a second that since God is the Creator, He can use any of His Creation, such as the wind, the rain, the oceans, tidal waves, tornadoes, hurricanes, earthquakes, anything He created to begin with to get the job done. Sure you can prove how it works, you can predict when a hurricane is forming, you can tell how the hurricane begins to form, but the thing you keep forgetting is that God created it to begin with and He can make it do as He wants**

for whatever He wants. He initially starts what you call 'the chain reaction' to begin with so all the rest of the elements fall right into place when He wants them to. He controls the speed of the wind, the direction the wind goes, sure He uses the moon and the sun to do that. He created those thing to control that. The farther and more in dept you want to research, there is always another item that goes beyond what you discover and what you can control or predict, yet God controls that item as well) which I will do in the midst thereof: and after that he (the king of Egypt) will let you go (the children of Israel). (God actually telling Moses when the king of Egypt will allow the children of Israel to leave)

21) And I will give this people favour in the sight of the Egyptians: and it shall come to pass, that, when ye go, ye shall not go empty.

22) But every woman shall borrow of her neighbour, and of her that sojourned (lived) in her house, jewels of silver, and jewels of gold, and raiment: and ye (you) shall put them upon your sons, and upon your daughters; and ye (you) shall spoil the Egyptians (leave the Egyptians and Egypt in poverty).

Exodus 4:1-31

1) And Moses answered and said, But, behold, they will not (no one will) believe me, nor hearken (listen) unto my voice: for they will say, The LORD hath not appeared unto thee. (even Moses had doubts at first)

2) And the LORD said unto him (Moses), What is that in thine hand? And he (Moses) said, A rod.

3) And he (God) said, Cast it (the rod) on the ground. And he (Moses) cast it (the rod) on the ground, and it (the rod) became a serpent; and Moses fled from before it (the serpent).

4) And the LORD said unto Moses, Put forth thine hand, and take it by the tail. And he (Moses) put forth his hand, and caught it (the serpent), and it (the serpent) became a rod in his (Moses) hand:

5) That they (the children of Israel) may believe that the LORD

God of their fathers, the God of Abraham, the God of Isaac, and the God of Jacob, hath appeared unto thee.

6) And the LORD said furthermore unto him (Moses), Put now thine (your) hand into thy (your) bosom. And he (Moses) put his hand into his bosom: and when he (Moses) took it (his hand) out, behold, his hand was leprous as snow.

7) And he (God) said, Put thine (your) hand into thy (your) bosom again. And he (Moses) put his hand into his bosom again; and plucked (took) it out of his bosom, and, behold, it (his hand) was turned again as his other flesh.

8) And it shall come to pass, if they (the children of Israel) will not believe thee (you), neither hearken (nor listen) to the voice of the first sign, that they (the children of Israel) will believe the voice of the latter sign.

9) And it shall come to pass, if they will not believe also these two signs, neither hearken unto thy (listen to your) voice, that thou (you) shalt take of the water of the river, and pour it upon the dry land: and the water which thou takest out of the river shall become blood upon the dry land.

10) And Moses said unto the LORD, O my LORD, I am not eloquent [1. speaking or spoken beautifully and forcefully: said or saying something in a forceful, expressive, and persuasive way. 2. expressing emotion clearly: expressing a feeling or thought clearly, memorably, or movingly. (Encarta ® World English Dictionary © & (P) 1998-2004 Microsoft Corporation. All rights reserved.)] neither heretofore, nor since thou hast (you have) spoken unto thy (your) servant: but I am slow of speech, and of a slow tongue. (this sounds like me until I get going and the Holy Spirit takes control of my tongue, then watch out. I don't hold back)

11) And the LORD said unto him (Moses), Who hath made man's mouth? or who maketh the dumb, or deaf, or the seeing, or the blind? have not I the LORD?

12) Now therefore go, and I will be with thy (your) mouth, and teach thee what thou shalt say. (Teach you what you need to say)

13) And he (Moses) said, O my LORD, send, I pray thee (ask you), by the hand of him (the one) whom thou wilt send (who

you will send).

14) And the anger of the LORD was kindled against Moses (see, Heavenly Angel Lay Lay said God got angry, here is yet another example of God getting angry. We are made in His image, it's human to get angry and to express that anger. No matter what secular counselor may say), and he (God) said, Is not Aaron the Levite thy brother? I know that he (Aaron) can speak well. And also, behold, he (Aaron) cometh forth to meet thee: and when he (Aaron) seeth thee, he will be glad in his heart.

15) And thou shalt (you will) speak unto him (Aaron), and put words in his mouth (tell him what to say): and I will be with thy mouth, and with his mouth, and will teach you what ye shall do.

16) And he shall be thy (your) spokesman unto the people: and he (Aaron) shall be, even he (Aaron) shall be to thee instead of a mouth (Aaron will be Moses mouth), and thou shalt be to him (Moses will tell Aaron what to say) instead of God.

17) And thou (you) shalt take this rod in thine (your) hand, wherewith thou (you) shalt do signs.

18) And Moses went and returned to Jethro his father in law, and said unto him, Let me go, I pray thee, and return unto my brethren which are in Egypt, and see whether they be yet alive. And Jethro said to Moses, Go in peace.

19) And the LORD said unto Moses in Midian, Go, return into Egypt: for all the men are dead which sought thy (your) life.

20) And Moses took his wife and his sons, and set them upon an ass, and he returned to the land of Egypt: and Moses took the rod of God in his hand.

21) And the LORD said unto Moses, When thou goest (you go) to return into Egypt, see that thou do all those wonders (miracles) before Pharaoh, which I have put in thine (your) hand: but I will harden his (Pharaoh's) heart, that he (Pharaoh) shall not let the people go.

22) And thou shalt say unto Pharaoh, Thus saith the LORD, Israel is my son, even my firstborn:

23) And I say unto thee (you), Let my son go, that he (the nation of Israel) may serve me: and if thou refuse to let him (Israel) go, behold, I will slay thy (your) son, even thy (your) firstborn.

24) And it came to pass by the way in the inn (eventually), that the LORD met him (the first born of the king of Egypt), and sought to kill him (the first born of the king of Egypt).

25) Then Zipporah took a sharp stone, and cut off the foreskin of her son (Gershom, Moses son), and cast it (the foreskin) at his (Moses) feet, and said, Surely a bloody husband art thou to me.

26) So he (Moses) let him go (Gershom): then she (Zipporah) said, A bloody husband thou art (Moses is), because of the circumcision. (now you know as well as I do, Moses and his wife, Zipporah are having an argument right now. Screaming and yelling at each other. Zipporah is really angry with Moses and Moses is 'putting his foot down' to Zipporah, his wife to let their son, Gershom go. If you cant see that, you don't want to see that. Just like Heavenly Angel Lay Lay said, Even the Prophets and Apostles got angry and had tempers, just like we do today)

27) And the LORD said to Aaron, Go into the wilderness to meet Moses. And he (Aaron) went, and met him (Moses) in the mount of God, and kissed him (Moses).

28) And Moses told Aaron all the words of the LORD who had sent him, and all the signs which he (God) had commanded him (Moses).

29) And Moses and Aaron went and gathered together all the elders of the children of Israel:

30) And Aaron spake all the words which the LORD had spoken unto Moses, and did the signs in the sight of the people.

31) And the people believed: and when they (the children of Israel) heard that the LORD had visited the children of Israel, and that he (the Lord) had looked upon their (the children of Israel's) affliction, then they (the children of Israel) bowed their heads and worshipped.

Exodus 5:1-23

1) And afterward Moses and Aaron went in, and told Pharaoh, Thus saith the LORD God of Israel, Let my people go, that they may hold a feast unto me in the wilderness.

2) And Pharaoh said, Who is the LORD, that I should obey his

voice to let Israel go? I know not the LORD, neither will I let Israel go.

3) And they (Moses and Aaron) said, The God of the Hebrews hath met with us: let us go, we pray thee, three days' journey into the desert, and sacrifice unto the LORD our God; lest (or else) he (the LORD) fall upon us with pestilence [1. med epidemic of disease: an epidemic of a highly contagious or infectious disease such as bubonic plague 2. med disease: a serious infectious disease 3. something evil: a malevolent belief, influence, or presence (Encarta ® World English Dictionary © & (P) 1998-2004 Microsoft Corporation. All rights reserved.)], or with the sword.

4) And the king of Egypt said unto them, Wherefore do ye, Moses and Aaron, let the people from their works? get you unto your burdens.

5) And Pharaoh said, Behold, the people of the land now are many, and ye (you) make them rest from their burdens (work).

6) And Pharaoh commanded the same day the taskmasters (supervisors) of the people, and their officers, saying,

7) Ye (you) shall no more give the people straw to make brick, as heretofore: let them (the people) go and gather straw for themselves.

8) And the tale of (the amount of) the bricks, which they (children of Israel) did make heretofore, ye (you) shall lay upon them (make them do); ye (you) shall not diminish (lessen) ought thereof: for they be idle (not doing anything); therefore they cry, saying, Let us go and sacrifice to our God.

9) Let there more work be laid upon the men (increase the men's work), that they may labour therein; and let them (the men) not regard (not listen to) vain words (what Moses and Aaron say).

10) And the taskmasters (supervisors) of the people went out, and their officers, and they (the supervisors) spake (spoke) to the people, saying, Thus saith Pharaoh, I will not give you straw.

11) Go ye (you go), get you straw where ye can find it: yet not ought of your work shall be diminished (the amount of your work shall be the same).

12) So the people (children of Israel) were scattered abroad

throughout all the land of Egypt to gather stubble instead of straw. (I had to stop and think about this scripture. Remember what Heavenly Angel Lay Lay said about stopping and thinking about what we are reading. What caught my eye was 'were scattered abroad throughout all the land of Egypt to gather stubble instead of straw'. Egypt is a pretty big country, just at a glance it's well over 2000 square miles which is 3340 square kilometers. How would the children of Israel travel so far and back in a day's time and not pick up straw, but stubble and still keep the amount of bricks they make each day up to the amount required by the king of Egypt? **The Israelites had even less to work with and had to do the same exact job. God made a way for the Israelites to do their job successfully**)

13) And the taskmasters (supervisors) hasted them (made the children of Israel hurry), saying, Fulfil your works (the amount of daily bricks), your daily tasks, as when there was straw.

14) And the officers of the children of Israel, which Pharaoh's taskmasters (supervisors) had set over them (the children of Israel), were beaten, and demanded, Wherefore have ye not fulfilled your task in making brick both yesterday and to day, as heretofore? (the children of Israel were falling behind in their daily task of the amount of bricks they were supposed to make)

15) Then the officers (leaders) of the children of Israel came and cried unto Pharaoh, saying, Wherefore dealest thou thus with thy servants?

16) There is no straw given unto thy (your) servants, and they (the supervisors) say to us, Make brick: and, behold, thy (your) servants are beaten; but the fault is in thine (your) own people.

17) But he (the Pharaoh) said, Ye are idle, ye are idle (you are not doing anything): therefore ye say, Let us go and do sacrifice to the LORD.

18) Go therefore now, and work; for there shall no straw be given you, yet shall ye deliver the tale (same amount) of bricks.

19) And the officers of the children of Israel did see that they were in evil case (they were in trouble), after it was said, Ye shall not minish (lessen) ought (their duty) from your bricks of your daily task.

20) And they (the officers of the children of Israel) met Moses and Aaron, who stood in the way, as they (the officers of the children of Israel) came forth from Pharaoh:

21) And they (the officers of the children of Israel) said unto them (Moses and Aaron), The LORD look upon you, and judge; because ye (you) have made our savour (the LORD) to be abhorred (strongly disliked) in the eyes of Pharaoh, and in the eyes of his (the Pharaoh's) servants, to put a sword in their (the Pharaoh's servants) hand to slay us (the officers of the children of Israel).

22) And Moses returned unto the LORD, and said, LORD, wherefore (why) hast (have) thou (you) so evil entreated this people? why is it that thou (you) hast (have) sent me?

23) For since I came to Pharaoh to speak in thy (your) name, he (the Pharaoh) hath done evil to this people (the children of Israel); neither hast thou delivered thy people at all (nor have you delivered the children of Israel at all). (now if you think Moses wasn't upset with God, you're kidding yourself. **Moses did exactly what God told Moses to do and the Pharaoh turned up the pressure on the children of Israel instead of releasing them and God hasn't delivered the children of Israel out of the land of Egypt as He promised either. Moses is wanting to know why. Everything is getting worse instead of better. We aren't to rely on our own understanding but 'every word of the living God. There is always a reason even though that reason is beyond our human understanding when we trust Him. Later we may find out what the 'whole picture' is)**

Exodus 6:1-30

1) Then the LORD said unto Moses, Now shalt thou see what I will do to Pharaoh: for with a strong hand shall he (Pharaoh) let them (the children of Israel) go, and with a strong hand shall he (Pharaoh) drive them (the children of Israel) out of his (Pharaoh's) land.

2) And God spake unto Moses, and said unto him (Moses), I am the LORD:

3) And I appeared (Right here, scriptures actually say **GOD APPEARED** to all three men. This also tells me the men back in the Old Testament had even conscious minds that were able to comprehend more Supernatural Power than our conscious minds can today. **When I saw the Silver Platter of purple grapes that appeared in Jesus hands, as magnificent as that was, those colors were still Earthly Colors compared to the Supernatural Colors when I saw Jesus 'Fiery Red Eyes' and the 'Hem of Jesus Throne Room Robe'. Those Heavenly Colors had to turn to black and white so they wouldn't hurt my human conscious mind. When I did get a glimpse of Jesus Himself standing patiently at the doorway to His Throne Room, I was only allowed to see Him in black and white because of the magnificence of the Supernatural Colors. There is more about this in my book MATTHEW'S WORD 'TWO':REAL WORD OF GOD BIBLE**) unto Abraham, unto Isaac, and unto Jacob, by the name of God Almighty, but by my name JEHOVAH was I not known to them.
4) And I have also established my covenant with them (Abraham, Isaac, and Jacob. To four generations), to give them (the descendants of Abraham, Isaac, and Jacob) the land of Canaan, the land of their pilgrimage, wherein they were strangers.
5) And I have also heard the groaning of the children of Israel, whom the Egyptians keep in bondage; and I have remembered (God doesn't forget, but does like to be reminded. This is His way of saying, 'it's time to continue keeping my promise to them. In human terms, this would be the same as withholding a gift that has been promised to us until we are able to handle the gift promised. Whether that gift is going to be reaped by us or our children or our children's children or their children) my covenant.
6) Wherefore say unto the children of Israel, I am the LORD, and I will bring you out from under the burdens of the Egyptians, and I will rid you out of their bondage, and I will redeem you with a stretched out arm (His Supernatural Power), and with great judgments (His judgments against Egypt):
7) And I will take you to me for a people, and I will be to you a

God (notice the word usage God uses here? 'to you a God', the children of Israel were in Egypt so long, some of them started worshipping 'false gods', 'idolism', in today's terms, as Heavenly Angel Lay Lay said, 'even sports and children are gods to men and women in today's society. Whatever or whoever a person puts first in their lives is their 'religion and their god'. God wants the children of Israel to worship Him the way the children of Israel worshipped the 'false idols of Egypt'): and ye shall know that I am the LORD your God, which bringeth you out from under the burdens of the Egyptians.

8) And I will bring you in unto the land (Canaan), concerning the which I did swear (promise) to give it to Abraham, to Isaac, and to Jacob; and I will give it you for an heritage: I am the LORD.

9) And Moses spake so unto (told) the children of Israel: but they hearkened not (did not listen) unto Moses for anguish of spirit (their spirit was beaten down), and for cruel bondage (no self-image or self-esteem, the children of Israel felt unworthy of any gift God had for them).

10) And the LORD spake unto Moses, saying,

11) Go in, speak unto Pharaoh king of Egypt, that he (Pharaoh) let the children of Israel go out of his land.

12) And Moses spake before the LORD, saying, Behold, the children of Israel have not hearkened unto me (have not listened to me); how then shall Pharaoh hear me, who am of uncircumcised lips? (why would the Pharaoh listen to Moses when the children of Israel doesn't even listen to Moses. Pharaoh doesn't fear God and the children of Israel do fear God)

13) And the LORD spake unto Moses and unto Aaron, and gave them a charge (put Moses and Aaron in charge of) unto the children of Israel, and unto Pharaoh king of Egypt, to bring the children of Israel out of the land of Egypt. (God didn't just put Moses and Aaron in charge of the children of Israel, but also God put Moses and Aaron in charge of Pharaoh, the king of Egypt as well)

14) These be the heads of their fathers' houses: The sons of Reuben the firstborn of Israel; Hanoch, and Pallu, Hezron, and Carmi: these be the families of Reuben.

15) And the sons of Simeon; Jemuel, and Jamin, and Ohad, and Jachin, and Zohar, and Shaul the son of a Canaanitish woman: these are the families of Simeon.

16) And these are the names of the sons of Levi according to their generations; Gershon, and Kohath, and Merari: and the years of the life of Levi were an hundred thirty and seven years (137).

17) The sons of Gershon; Libni, and Shimi, according to their families.

18) And the sons of Kohath; Amram, and Izhar, and Hebron, and Uzziel: and the years of the life of Kohath were an hundred thirty and three years (133).

19) And the sons of Merari; Mahali and Mushi: these are the families of Levi according to their generations.

20) And Amram took him Jochebed his father's sister to wife; and she bare him Aaron and Moses (Notice: Aaron is older than Moses. Aaron was first born): and the years of the life of Amram were an hundred and thirty and seven years (137).

21) And the sons of Izhar; Korah, and Nepheg, and Zichri.

22) And the sons of Uzziel; Mishael, and Elzaphan, and Zithri.

23) And Aaron took him Elisheba, daughter of Amminadab, sister of Naashon, to wife; and she bare him Nadab, and Abihu, Eleazar, and Ithamar.

24) And the sons of Korah; Assir, and Elkanah, and Abiasaph: these are the families of the Korhites.

25) And Eleazar Aaron's son took him one of the daughters of Putiel to wife; and she bare him (Eleazar) Phinehas: these are the heads of the fathers of the Levites according to their families.

26) These are that Aaron and Moses, to whom the LORD said, Bring out the children of Israel from the land of Egypt according to their armies.

27) These are they (Aaron and Moses spoke on behalf of all the Israelites) which spake to Pharaoh king of Egypt, to bring out the children of Israel from Egypt: these (all these souls and their families) are that Moses and Aaron.

28) And it came to pass on the day when the LORD spake (spoke) unto Moses in the land of Egypt,

29) That the LORD spake (spoke) unto Moses, saying, I am the LORD: speak thou unto Pharaoh king of Egypt all that I say unto thee (to you).

30) And Moses said before the LORD, Behold, I am of uncircumcised lips, and how shall Pharaoh hearken (listen) unto me?

Exodus 7:1-25

1) And the LORD said unto Moses, See, I have made thee (you) a god to Pharaoh (why only A god? Pharaoh didn't believe in only one god, remember? Pharaoh believed in several different gods. So Moses was A god to Pharaoh): and Aaron thy (your) brother shall be thy (your) prophet (talk about a raise in status. God made Moses a god to the strongest Earthly King at that time and Aaron was the prophet for Moses. This reminds me of when I took Damien, the King of Satanism on and backed him down. Being a child of the Most High God, I outrank the King of Satanism and Damien knew it. More about this in my book MATTHEW'S WORD 'TWO':REAL WORD OF GOD BIBLE. Moses being a child of the Most High God outranked the Pharaoh and the Pharaoh was about to find that out)

2) Thou (you) shalt (will) speak all that I command thee (you): and Aaron thy (your) brother shall speak unto Pharaoh, that he (Pharaoh) send the children of Israel out of his (the Pharaoh's) land.

3) And I will harden Pharaoh's heart, and multiply my signs and my wonders in the land of Egypt. (I often wondered why God hardened Pharaoh's heart so the Pharaoh wouldn't let the children of Israel go. Well, the answer is that if the Pharaoh would have allowed the children of Israel go the first time Moses talked to Pharaoh, then the Pharaoh wouldn't have learned a lesson, and neither would the Israelites. The Pharaoh would have believed the Pharaoh could go get the Israelites any time the Pharaoh wanted the Israelites back. God wanted the Israelites free, once and for all. The Israelites on the other hand wouldn't have seen the wondrous miracles from God if the Pharaoh would

have released the Israelites right away.   The Israelites also wouldn't have learned to trust and depend on God as their ancestors did.   The Israelites would have gotten into trouble and wanted to return to the Pharaoh instead of trusting in God.)

4) But Pharaoh shall not hearken unto (listen to) you, that I may lay my hand upon Egypt (God wanted to teach everyone a lesson, not just the Pharaoh, and not just the children of Israel), and bring forth mine armies, and my people the children of Israel, out of the land of Egypt by great judgments.

5) And the Egyptians shall know that I am the LORD, when I stretch forth mine hand upon Egypt, and bring out the children of Israel from among them.

6) And Moses and Aaron did as the LORD commanded them (Moses and Aaron), so did they (this is reaffirming that Moses and Aaron did as God commanded them to do).

7) And Moses was fourscore years old (80 years old), and Aaron fourscore and three years old (83 years old) (See, Aaron is the oldest, yet God chose Moses to free the Israelites), when they spake unto (**Aaron and Moses spoke to)** Pharaoh. (**Aaron was a 'follower' even though God used Aaron as a 'leader' for a short time. Aaron allowed the children of Israel to persuade him to make a 'graven image' in the desert and Aaron followed Miriam when Miriam spoke out against Moses too. Just like Heavenly Angel Lay Lay said, 'All God needs is a willing vessel', more about this subject in my book MATTHEW'S WORD 'TWO':REAL WORD OF GOD BIBLE**)

8) And the LORD spake unto Moses and unto Aaron, saying,

9) When Pharaoh shall speak unto you, saying, Shew a miracle for you: then thou shalt **say unto Aaron**, Take thy rod, and cast it before Pharaoh, and it (the rod) shall become a serpent.

10) And Moses and Aaron went in unto Pharaoh, and they (Moses and Aaron) did so as the LORD had commanded: **and Aaron cast down his rod before Pharaoh, and before his servants, and it (the rod) became a serpent. (Aaron is doing the actions)**

11) Then Pharaoh also called the wise men (astrologers) and the

sorcerers ('Wicca or white magic'): now the magicians ('Wicca or white magic') of Egypt, they (the Wicca) also did in like manner with their enchantments (this is what Heavenly Angel Lay Lay was talking about, 'saying the words to cast a spell'. More about this subject in my book MATTHEW'S WORD 'TWO':REAL WORD OF GOD BIBLE)

12) For they (the sorcerers) cast down every man his rod, and they (their rods) became serpents: but Aaron's rod swallowed up their rods. **(the Spiritual Battle of Good and Evil begin again)**

13) And he (the Lord) hardened Pharaoh's heart, that he hearkened not (the Pharaoh did not listen) unto them; as the LORD had said.

14) And the LORD said unto Moses, Pharaoh's heart is hardened, he (the Pharaoh) refuseth (refuses) to let the people go.

15) Get thee (go) unto Pharaoh in the morning; lo, he goeth out unto the water; and thou shalt (you shall) stand by the river's brink against he come (on the other side); and the rod which was turned to a serpent shalt thou take in thine hand.

16) And thou shalt say unto him (the Pharaoh), The LORD God of the Hebrews hath sent me unto thee (you), saying, Let my people go, that they may serve me in the wilderness: and, behold, hitherto thou (before you) wouldest not hear.

17) Thus saith the LORD, In this thou shalt know that I am the LORD: behold, I will smite (afflict) with the rod that is in mine hand upon the waters which are in the river, and they (the waters in the river) shall be turned to blood.

18) And the fish that is in the river shall die, and the river shall stink; and the Egyptians shall lothe to drink (unwilling to drink) of the water of the river.

19) And the LORD spake unto Moses, **Say unto Aaron**, Take thy rod, and stretch out thine hand upon the waters of Egypt, upon their streams, upon their rivers, and upon their ponds, and upon all their pools of water, that they may become blood; and that there may be blood throughout all the land of Egypt, both in vessels of wood, and in vessels of stone. (God didn't stop with just the rivers and ponds of Egypt, He even contaminated all the water in the water vessels as well. Aaron is still the go between.)

20) And Moses and Aaron did so, as the LORD commanded; and he (Aaron) lifted up the rod, and smote (afflicted) the waters that were in the river, in the sight of Pharaoh, and in the sight of his servants; and all the waters that were in the river were turned to blood.   (Every movie I have ever watched about the 'Ten Commandments' shows Moses doing all these things. Well, It's really Aaron doing all these things. Remember what Heavenly Angel Lay Lay said about Hollywood?   Don't believe what Hollywood puts out, Hollywood is owned by Satan and down plays the King James Version of the Word of God)

21) And the fish that was in the river died (apparently there is no air in stale blood. The fish died, there wasn't enough air for even the fish to survive); and the river stank (stale blood stinks), and the Egyptians could not drink of the water of the river; and there was blood throughout all the land of Egypt.

22) And the magicians of Egypt did so with their enchantments. (Satan doesn't give up even one soul without a fight, but we keep at it, Satan always looses):   and Pharaoh's heart was hardened, neither did he (Pharaoh) hearken (listen) unto them (Moses and Aaron); as the LORD had said.

23) And Pharaoh turned and went into his (Pharaoh's) house, neither did he (Pharaoh) set his (Pharaoh's) heart to this also.

24) And all the Egyptians digged round about the river for water to drink; for they could not drink of the water of the river. (the Egyptians started digging wells that were close to the river for fresh water)

25) And seven days were fulfilled (a whole week without water), after that the LORD had smitten (affected) the river.

Exodus 8:1-32

1) And the LORD spake unto Moses, Go unto Pharaoh, and say unto him (Pharaoh), Thus saith the LORD, Let my people go, that they (the children of Israel) may serve me.

2) And if thou (the Pharaoh) refuse to let them (the children of Israel) go, behold, I will smite (afflict) all thy borders (the borders of Egypt) with frogs:

3) And the river shall bring forth frogs abundantly, which shall go up and come into thine (your) house, and into thy bedchamber, and upon thy bed, and into the house of thy servants, and upon thy people, and into thine ovens, and into thy kneadingtroughs:

4) And the frogs shall come up both on thee (the Pharaoh), and upon thy (the Pharaoh's) people, and upon all thy (the Pharaoh's) servants.

5) And the LORD spake unto Moses, **Say unto Aaron**, Stretch forth thine (your) hand with thy (your) rod over the streams, over the rivers, and over the ponds, and cause frogs to come up upon the land of Egypt.

6) And **Aaron stretched out his hand over the waters of Egypt; and the frogs came up, and covered the land of Egypt.** (See? Aaron is the one who stretches forth his hand again, not Moses)

7) And the magicians did so with their enchantments, and brought up frogs upon the land of Egypt. (So far we have 'Good vs. Evil' comparing powers)

8) Then Pharaoh called for Moses and Aaron, and said, Intreat (plead with) the LORD, that he (the Lord) may take away the frogs from me, and from my people; and I will let the people (the Israelites) go, that they (the Israelites) may do sacrifice unto the LORD.

9) And Moses said unto Pharaoh, Glory over me: when shall I intreat (ask) for thee (you), and for thy (your) servants, and for thy (your) people, to destroy the frogs from thee (you) and thy (your) houses, that they (the frogs) may remain in the river only?

10) And he (Pharaoh) said, To morrow. And he (Moses) said, Be it according to thy (the Pharaoh's) word: that thou (the Pharaoh) mayest know that there is none like unto the LORD our God. (See? God is teaching everyone a lesson on who is the Most High God)

11) And the frogs shall depart from thee (Pharaoh), and from thy (Pharaoh's) houses, and from thy (Pharaoh's) servants, and from thy (Pharaoh's) people; they (the frogs) shall remain in the river only.

12) And Moses and Aaron went out from Pharaoh: and Moses cried unto the LORD because of the frogs which he (God) had brought against Pharaoh.

13) And the LORD did according to the word of Moses; and the frogs died out of the houses, out of the villages, and out of the fields.

14) And they (the people) gathered them (the frogs) together upon heaps: and the land stank.

15) But when Pharaoh saw that there was respite (relief from the frogs), he (Pharaoh) hardened his heart, and hearkened not (did not listen to) unto them (went back on his word); as the LORD had said.

16) And the LORD said unto Moses, **Say unto Aaron**, (have you noticed, every time God wants Moses to do something God says, 'Say unto Aaron', there is no room for confusion) Stretch out thy rod, and smite (afflict) the dust of the land, that it may become lice throughout all the land of Egypt.

17) And they (Moses and Aaron) did so; for **Aaron stretched out his** (Aaron's) **hand with his rod**, and smote (afflicted) the dust of the earth, and it (the dust) (remember in MATTHEW'S WORD 'TWO':REAL WORD OF GOD BIBLE, Heavenly Angel Lay Lay said, 'God still does create, it's just that human's don't know what to look for. Here is a good example of God still creating. The scriptures say, 'it', meaning 'the dust' turned to lice. We just don't know what to look for) became lice in man, and in beast; all the dust of the land became lice throughout all the land of Egypt (There it is again, 'all the dust of the land became lice throughout the land of Egypt'. The dust turned to lice. God created lice out of dust) (Aaron does the actions again, Aaron stretched out his hand, not Moses)

18) And the magicians did so with their enchantments to bring forth lice, but they could not (the magicians failed): so there were lice upon man, and upon beast. (God is starting to distinguish which God is most powerful now)

19) Then the magicians said unto Pharaoh, This is the finger of God (now the magicians believe): and Pharaoh's heart was hardened, and he (Pharaoh) hearkened not unto (did not listen to)

them; as the LORD had said.

20) And **the LORD said unto Moses**, Rise up early in the morning, and stand before Pharaoh; lo, he (Pharaoh) cometh forth to the water; and **say unto him (the Pharaoh)**, Thus saith the LORD, Let my people (the children of Israel) go, that they (the children of Israel) may serve me (the Most High God) (**Moses did this one on his own, without Aaron being involved**).

21) Else, if thou wilt not (the Pharaoh will not) let my people (the children of Israel) go, behold, I will send swarms of flies upon thee (Pharaoh), and upon thy (Pharaoh's) servants, and upon thy (Pharaoh's) people, and into thy (Pharaoh's) houses: and the houses of the Egyptians shall be full of swarms of flies, and also the ground whereon they (the houses) are.

22) And I will sever (separate) in that day the land of Goshen, in which my people dwell (live), that no swarms of flies shall be there; to the end thou mayest know that I am the LORD in the midst of the earth. (Now God is going to do something Supernatural again. All the flies are going to be in the borders of Egypt and not one fly will be in the land of Goshen. Goshen is in Egypt, so picture it this way. There is one spot in acres and acres of land that no fly will be in where in all the rest of all those acres of land, flies will be monstrous. Goshen is where the Israelites lived and Joseph was buried, within the Egyptian borders)

23) And I will put a division between my people (the Israelites) and thy people (the Egyptians): to morrow shall this sign be.

24) And the LORD did so; and there came a grievous swarm of flies into the house of Pharaoh, and into his (Pharaoh's) servants' houses, and into all the land of Egypt: the land was corrupted by reason of the swarm of flies.

25) And Pharaoh called for Moses and for Aaron, and said, Go ye, sacrifice to your God in the land.

26) And **Moses said, It is not meet so to do** (no sacrifices can be made in Egypt); **for we shall sacrifice the abomination of the Egyptians to the LORD our God: lo, shall we sacrifice the abomination of the Egyptians before their eyes, and will they not stone us?** (The Egyptians would stone the Israelites for sacrificing to God)

27) **We will go three days' journey into the wilderness, and sacrifice to the LORD our God, as he (God) shall command us.** (guess what? Moses is speaking to Pharaoh now on his own, without Aaron speaking for Moses. Moses self-image is going up even more now. What's changing? The time all these miracles are happening are not back to back. I did a report on this in college. All the miracles that happened took about eight years from the first to the last. During that time Moses was reading God's Word and listening and studying, along with seeing the miracles with his own two eyes)

28) And Pharaoh said, I will let you go, that ye (you) may sacrifice to the LORD your God in the wilderness; only ye (you) shall not go very far away (the Pharaoh is afraid of loosing his slaves): intreat (ask your God on my behalf) for me.

29) And Moses said, Behold, I go out from thee (Pharaoh), and I will intreat (ask) the LORD that the swarms of flies may depart from Pharaoh, from his (Pharaoh's) servants, and from his (Pharaoh's) people, to morrow: but let not Pharaoh deal deceitfully any more in not letting the people (Israelites) go to sacrifice to the LORD.

30) And Moses went out from Pharaoh, and intreated (asked) the LORD.

31) And the LORD did according to the word of Moses; and he (God) removed the swarms of flies from Pharaoh, from his (Pharaoh's) servants, and from his (Pharaoh's) people; there remained not one.

32) And Pharaoh hardened his heart at this time also (changed his mind again) (See what happens if you change your mind after you say you will do something and don't do it?), neither would he (the Pharaoh) let the people (the children of Israel) go.

Exodus 9:1-35

1) Then **the LORD said unto Moses**, (God didn't tell Aaron this time, just Moses) Go in unto Pharaoh, and tell him (Pharaoh), Thus saith the LORD God of the Hebrews, Let my people (children of Israel) go, that they (the children of Israel) may serve

me (God).

2) For if thou (Pharaoh) refuse to let them (children of Israel) go, and wilt hold them still (continue to hold the children of Israel in Egypt),

3) Behold, the hand of the LORD is upon thy (your) cattle which is in the field, upon the horses, upon the asses, upon the camels, upon the oxen, and upon the sheep: there shall be a very grievous murrain (plagues and diseases on the animals).

4) And the LORD shall sever between (divide) the cattle of Israel and the cattle of Egypt: and there shall nothing die of all that is the children's of Israel.

5) And the LORD appointed a set time (God starts putting time limits on things here), saying, To morrow the LORD shall do this thing in the land.

6) And the LORD did that thing on the morrow, and all the cattle of Egypt died: but of the cattle of the children of Israel died not one.

7) And Pharaoh sent, and, behold, there was not one of the cattle of the Israelites dead. And the heart of Pharaoh was hardened, and he (the Pharaoh) did not let the people (Israelites) go.

8) And **the LORD said unto Moses and unto Aaron** (now Aaron is back in the picture again), Take to you handfuls of ashes of the furnace, **and let Moses sprinkle it** (now God is telling Moses to sprinkle the ashes along with Aaron. Moses self-esteem is still growing, not needing Aaron as much as Moses did before) toward the heaven in the sight of Pharaoh (while Pharaoh watches).

9) And it (the ashes) shall become small dust in all the land of Egypt, and shall be a boil breaking forth with blains (swelling or boils) upon man, and upon beast, throughout all the land of Egypt. (No movie ever showed this either)

10) And they (Moses and Aaron both take part in this, not just Aaron) took ashes of the furnace, and stood before Pharaoh; and Moses sprinkled it (the ashes) up toward heaven; and it (the ashes) became a boil breaking forth with blains upon man, and upon beast.

11) And the magicians could not stand before Moses because of

the boils; for the boil was upon the magicians (even the magicians had boils on them) , and upon all the Egyptians.

12) And the LORD hardened the heart of Pharaoh, and he (Pharaoh) hearkened not unto (did not listen to) them Moses and Aaron); as the LORD had spoken unto Moses.

13) And the LORD said unto Moses, Rise up early in the morning, and stand before Pharaoh, and say unto him (Pharaoh), Thus saith the LORD God of the Hebrews, Let my people go (the Israelites), that they (the Israelites) may serve me (God).

14) For I will at this time send all my plagues upon thine heart (Pharaoh's heart), and upon thy (Pharaoh's) servants, and upon thy (Pharaoh's) people; that thou mayest know (Pharaoh will know) that there is none like me (God) in all the earth.

15) For now I (God) will stretch out my hand, that I may smite (afflict) thee (Pharaoh) and thy (Pharaoh's) people with pestilence; and thou (Pharaoh) shalt be cut off from the earth.

16) And in very deed for this cause (to prove that God is the Most High God) have I raised thee (Moses) up, for to shew (show) in thee (Moses) my (God's) power; and that my (God's) name may be declared throughout all the earth.

17) As yet exaltest thou thyself (Pharaoh puts himself above the children of Israel) against my people (Israelites), that thou wilt (you will) not let them (the Israelites) go?

18) Behold, to morrow about this time I will cause it (the weather) to rain a very grievous hail, such as hath not been in Egypt since the foundation thereof even until now. (Never before, not even since the creation of the Earth, until now)

19) Send therefore now, and gather thy (your) cattle, and all that thou hast (you have) in the field; for upon every man and beast which shall be found in the field, and shall not be brought home, the hail shall come down upon them (man and beast), and they (all that is not in the houses) shall die.

20) He (the men) that feared the word of the LORD among the servants of Pharaoh made his servants and his cattle flee into the houses: (even the servants of Pharaoh feared God and made their servants and animals come into the houses to save their lives)

21) And he (the men) that regarded not (did not believe) the word

of the LORD left his servants and his cattle in the field.

22) And the LORD said unto Moses, Stretch forth thine (your) hand toward heaven (Moses stretches forth his hand this time instead of Aaron), that there may be hail in all the land of Egypt, upon man, and upon beast, and upon every herb of the field, throughout the land of Egypt. (Moses is getting even more self-esteem and self-image)

23) And Moses stretched forth his rod toward heaven (Moses does the action this time instead of Aaron): and the LORD sent thunder and hail, and the fire ran along upon the ground; and the LORD rained hail upon the land of Egypt.

24) So there was hail, and fire mingled with the hail, very grievous, such as there was none like it (no other weather like it) in all the land of Egypt since it (Egypt) became a nation.

25) And the hail smote (afflicted, killed) throughout all the land of Egypt all that was in the field, both man and beast; and the hail smote (broke) every herb of the field, and brake every tree of the field.

26) Only in the land of Goshen, where the children of Israel were, was there no hail. (God still saving the Israelites from harm, as long as they listen to Him and do as He says)

27) And Pharaoh sent, and called for Moses and Aaron, and said unto them (Moses and Aaron), I have sinned this time: the LORD is righteous, and I and my people are wicked.

28) Intreat (ask) the LORD (for it is enough) that there be no more mighty thunderings and hail; and I will let you go, and ye (you) shall stay no longer.

29) And Moses said unto him (Pharaoh), As soon as I am gone out of the city, I will spread abroad my hands unto the LORD; and the thunder shall cease, neither shall there be any more hail; that thou (you) mayest know how that the earth is the LORD's. **(Moses is still talking to Pharaoh instead of Aaron)**

30) But as for thee (you) and thy (your) servants, I know that ye (you) will not yet fear the LORD God.

31) And the flax and the barley was smitten (affected): for the barley was in the ear, and the flax was bolled (ruined).

32) But the wheat and the rie were not smitten (affected): for they

(wheat and rie) were not grown up.

33) And Moses went out of the city from Pharaoh, and spread abroad his (Moses) hands unto the LORD: and the thunders and hail ceased, and the rain was not poured upon the earth.

34) And when Pharaoh saw that the rain and the hail and the thunders were ceased, he (Pharaoh) sinned yet more, and hardened his (Pharaoh's) heart, he (Pharaoh) and his (Pharaoh's) servants.

35) And the heart of Pharaoh was hardened, neither would he (Pharaoh) let the children of Israel go; as the LORD had spoken by Moses. (Here is a good example of what Heavenly Angel Lay Lay said about when she said once the words are spoken they are law, if you 'change your mind', that's considered a sin.' The scripture 34 states, 'he sinned yet more', meaning Pharaoh changed his mind and went back on his word)

Exodus 10:1-29

1) And the LORD said unto Moses, Go in unto Pharaoh: for I have hardened his (Pharaoh's) heart, and the heart of his (Pharaoh's) servants, that I might shew these my signs before him (Pharaoh):

2) And that thou (you) mayest tell in the ears of thy (your) son, and of thy son's son, what things I have wrought (done) in Egypt, and my signs which I have done among them (the Israelites); that ye (you) may know how that I am the LORD.

3) And Moses and Aaron came in unto Pharaoh, and said unto him (Pharaoh), Thus saith the LORD God of the Hebrews, How long wilt thou refuse to humble thyself (yourself) before me (God)? let my people go, that they (the Israelites) may serve me (God).

4) Else, if thou (you) refuse to let my people go, behold, to morrow will I bring the locusts into thy (your) coast:

5) And they (the locust) shall cover the face of the earth, that one cannot be able to see the earth: and they (the locust) shall eat the residue of that which is escaped, which remaineth unto you from the hail, and shall eat every tree which groweth for you out of the

field: (what the hail didn't destroy, the locust will eat)

6) And they (the locust) shall fill thy (your) houses, and the houses of all thy (your) servants, and the houses of all the Egyptians; which neither thy (your) fathers, nor thy (your) fathers' fathers have seen, since the day that they (mankind) were upon the earth unto this day. And he (Moses) turned himself, and went out from Pharaoh.

7) And Pharaoh's servants said unto him (Pharaoh), How long shall this man be a snare unto us? let the men go, that they may serve the LORD their God: knowest thou not (don't you know) yet that Egypt is destroyed?

8) And Moses and Aaron were brought again unto Pharaoh: and he (Pharaoh) said unto them (Moses and Aaron), Go, serve the LORD your God: but who are they that shall go? (who all will be going?)

9) And **Moses said, We will go with our young and with our old, with our sons and with our daughters, with our flocks and with our herds will we go; for we must hold a feast unto the LORD**. (Moses is still talking to Pharaoh now instead of going through Aaron. Sounds like Moses self-worth is growing even more)

10) And he (Pharaoh) said unto them (Moses and Aaron), Let the LORD be so with you, as I will let you go, and your little ones: look to it; for evil is before you.

11) Not so: go now ye (you) that are men, and serve the LORD; for that ye (you) did desire. And they (Moses and Aaron) were driven out from Pharaoh's presence. (Pharaoh is only going to allow the men go and worship the Lord, not the women and children)

12) And the LORD said unto Moses, **Stretch out thine (your) hand over the land of Egypt for the locusts, that they (the locusts) may come up upon the land of Egypt, and eat every herb of the land, even all that the hail hath left.** (God is directly telling Moses to do the actions now instead of telling Moses to tell Aaron to do the actions)

13) And **Moses stretched forth his rod over the land of Egypt**, and the LORD brought an east wind upon the land all that day,

and all that night; and when it was morning, the east wind brought the locusts. (now I know why there is horrible fishing when there is an east wind. You can't catch anything with an east wind)

14) And the locust went up over all the land of Egypt, and rested in all the coasts of Egypt: very grievous were they (the locust); before them (the locusts) there were no such locusts as they (as there were then), neither after them shall be such (there will never be any such locusts as them after this either).

15) For they (the locusts) covered the face of the whole earth, so that the land was darkened; and they (the locusts) did eat every herb of the land, and all the fruit of the trees which the hail had left: and there remained not any green thing in the trees, or in the herbs of the field, through all the land of Egypt.

16) Then Pharaoh called for Moses and Aaron in haste (in a hurry); and he (Pharaoh) said, I have sinned against the LORD your God, and against you.

17) Now therefore forgive, I pray thee (ask you), my sin only this once, and intreat (ask, beg, plea with) the LORD your God, that he (your God) may take away from me (Pharaoh) this death only.

18) And he (Moses) went out from Pharaoh, and intreated (pleaded with) the LORD.

19) And the LORD turned a mighty strong west wind, which took away the locusts, and cast them into the Red sea; there remained not one locust in all the coasts of Egypt. (now I know why there is such good fishing during a west wind. Fish bite like crazy in a west wind)

20) But the LORD hardened Pharaoh's heart, so that he (Pharaoh) would not let the children of Israel go.

21) And **the LORD said unto Moses, Stretch out thine (your) hand toward heaven,** that there may be darkness over the land of Egypt, even darkness which may be felt (darkness feels cold, just like death).

22) And **Moses stretched forth his hand toward heaven**; and there was a thick darkness in all the land of Egypt three days: (**Moses is getting more self-confidence.** This sounds like the Earth stood still for three days straight. If the sun would have

stopped shining for three days straight everyone and everything would have frozen to death)

23) They (the people) saw not one another (could not see each other), neither rose any from his place for three days (the people couldn't move from one place to another, they couldn't see where they were going): but all the children of Israel had light in their dwellings.

24) And Pharaoh called unto Moses, and said, Go ye, serve the LORD; only let your flocks and your herds be stayed: let your little ones also go with you. (Pharaoh is still trying to keep something of the children of Israel's to make sure the children of Israel return to Egypt under slavery)

25) And Moses said, Thou (you) must give us also sacrifices and burnt offerings, that we may sacrifice unto the LORD our God.

26) Our cattle also shall go with us; there shall not an hoof be left behind; for thereof must we take to serve the LORD our God; and we know not with what we must serve the LORD, until we come thither. (Moses refusing to accept Pharaoh's offer of only half of what God wants done. All of us need to learn from this, hold out for ALL of what God wants us to have. Moses also doesn't know what God will want to be sacrificed yet; therefore, everything must go with the Israelites)

27) But the LORD hardened Pharaoh's heart (again Pharaoh refused to do as what is told to him), and he (Pharaoh) would not let them (the Israelites) go.

28) And Pharaoh said unto him (Moses), Get thee from me (get away from me), take heed to thyself (Pharaoh is warning Moses and Aaron), see my (Pharaoh's) face no more; for in that day thou seest (Moses or Aaron) my face (Pharaoh's face) thou (Moses and Aaron) shalt (will) die.

29) And Moses said, Thou (Pharaoh) hast (has) spoken well, I will see thy (Pharaoh's) face again no more. (Pharaoh has had enough, 'Pharaoh is at the end of his rope')

Exodus 11:1-10

1) And the LORD said unto Moses, Yet will I bring one plague

more upon Pharaoh, and upon Egypt; afterwards he (Pharaoh) will let you (the children of Israel) go hence (from here): when he (Pharaoh) shall let you go, he (Pharaoh) shall surely thrust you out hence altogether (will not only let the children of Israel go, Pharaoh will actually push the children of Israel out of Pharaoh's kingdom forever).

2) **Speak now in the ears of the people** (God is telling Moses to tell everyone, not to have Moses tell Aaron to tell everyone), and let every man borrow of his neighbour, and every woman of her neighbour, jewels of silver and jewels of gold. (Reading God's Real Word of God each day and over time, He builds our self worth)

3) And the LORD gave the people (the children of Israel) favour in the sight of the Egyptians (cultural status is changing, now the children of Israel are above the Egyptians). Moreover the man Moses was very great in the land of Egypt, in the sight of Pharaoh's servants, and in the sight of the people. (Moses was the leader of all, even the Egyptians)

4) And Moses said, Thus saith the LORD, About midnight will I go out into the midst of Egypt:

5) And all the firstborn in the land of Egypt shall die, from the first born of Pharaoh that sitteth upon his throne, even unto the firstborn of the maidservant that is behind the mill; and all the firstborn of beasts (not only the first born of the people, but also the animals).

6) And there shall be a great cry (grieving) throughout all the land of Egypt, such as there was none like it, nor shall be like it any more. (the grieving will be as there never was before nor will there be a grieving like this again)

7) But against any of the children of Israel shall not a dog move his tongue (no person or any beast will come against the children of Israel), against man or beast: that ye (you) may know how that the LORD doth (distinguishes, separates) put a difference between the Egyptians and Israel.

8) And all these thy (your) servants shall come down unto me (Moses), and bow down themselves unto me (Moses), saying, Get thee out (Moses will be commanded to leave Egypt), and all

the people that follow thee (all the people who follow Moses will be commanded to go with Moses and leave Egypt as well): and after that I will go out (that's when Moses will leave, with all the people who wish to leave with Moses). And **he** (Moses) **went out from Pharaoh in a great anger** (Moses is mad. Moses is angry, even serving God and doing all these miracles, Moses is still human and still shows his temper).

9) And the LORD said unto Moses, Pharaoh shall not hearken (listen) unto you; that my (God's) wonders may be multiplied in the land of Egypt.

10) And Moses and Aaron did all these wonders (miracles) before Pharaoh: and the LORD hardened Pharaoh's heart, so that he (Pharaoh) would not let the children of Israel go out of his (Pharaoh's) land (Egypt).

Exodus 12:1-51

1) And the LORD spake unto Moses and Aaron in the land of Egypt saying,

2) **This month shall be unto you the beginning of months: it shall be the first month of the year to you. (God is actually changing the calendar year here. Whatever month Egypt and Israel were in, this month is the beginning of a new year.** I wonder if any of those scholars have caught this scripture trying to date all those fossils that are supposed to be billions of years old when the fossils can't be over 35,000-40,000 years old. If you don't know what I'm talking about with these numbers, then you need to get my book MATTHEW'S WORD 'TWO':REAL WORD OF GOD BIBLE and read where Protecting Angel Shadow and Heavenly Angel Lay Lay GUESSED the actual age of the EARTH. Shadow and Lay Lay were both there when the Earth was Created, they are be able to give an estimated guess of the real age of the Earth since the Earth was created before time ever existed. Some scientist smarter than me needs to make a test to date back to 35,000-40,000 years old and use that test to date all those fossils, then everything would date correctly)

3) Speak ye (you) unto all the congregation of Israel, saying, In

the tenth day of this month they (Israel) shall take to them every man (each man who is the head of the household) a lamb, according to the house of their fathers, a lamb for an house:

4) And if the household be too little for the lamb, let him and his neighbour next unto his house take it according to the number of the souls (apparently there is one lamb for a certain number of people in each household); every man according to his eating shall make your count for the lamb.

5) Your lamb shall be without blemish, a male of the first year (only the first year lamb is accepted for offering to God. That's why Satanist's have a rams head as a symbol, a ram is more than a year old): ye (you) shall take it (the sacrifice) out from the sheep, or from the goats (the sacrifice doesn't matter whether it's a sheep or a goat as long as it's younger than a year old):

6) And **ye** (you) **shall keep it** (the sacrifice) **up** (not allow the sacrifice to sleep. At first I thought the scripture meant the sacrifice was supposed to hang after it was sacrificed for fourteen days, but the sacrifice isn't even sacrificed yet, it's still alive. It doesn't get sacrificed until the end of this verse) **until the fourteenth day of the same month**: and the whole assembly of the congregation of Israel shall kill it (their sacrifice. See? Now the sacrifice is dead) in the evening (a particular time God has set for the sacrifice to take place).

7) And they (each household of Israel) shall take of the blood, and strike it (the blood) on the two side posts and on the upper door post of the houses, wherein they (the household) shall eat it (now God is telling them, they will eat the lamb).

8) And they (the household of Israel) shall eat the flesh in that night (God is telling Israel when they are to eat of flesh of the sacrifice), roast with fire (God is telling Israel how to prepare the flesh of the sacrifice in order to eat the flesh), and unleavened bread (now God is telling Israel they are to eat the flesh if the sacrifice with unleavened bread and not just the flesh of the sacrifice alone); and with bitter herbs they shall eat it (the flesh of the sacrifice is to be cooked and eaten with bitter herbs, seasoning).

9) Eat not of it raw (God is warning the Israelites not to eat the

flesh raw), nor sodden at all (soaked in or saturated) with water, but roast with fire (God is re-emphasizing how the flesh is to be prepared and cooked, roasted with fire); his (the sacrifices) head with his legs, and with the purtenance (the innards or guts of the sacrifice still in the body) thereof. (this tells us the sacrifice must have it's throat slit and the blood drained out for the door posts. If the sacrifice was choked to death, there would not be any blood to put around the door posts and that is the only two ways I know of to kill and cook an animal with their innards still in their body) 10) And ye (you) shall let nothing of it (the sacrifice) remain until the morning; and that which remaineth of it until the morning (if any flesh remains until the morning) ye (you) shall burn with fire (burn whatever remains with fire to destroy it).

11) And thus shall ye (you) eat it (the flesh of the sacrifice); with your loins (the part of your back between your ribs and hip) girded (covered, protected), your shoes on your feet, and your staff in your hand; and ye (you) shall eat it (the flesh of the sacrifice) in haste (quickly): it (this night) is the LORD's passover. (now we know where the term, 'Passover' came from. Sounds like the Israelites are preparing for a war)

12) For I will pass through the land of Egypt this night, and will smite (kill) all the firstborn in the land of Egypt, both man and beast; and against all the gods of Egypt I will execute judgment: I am the LORD. (I would say God has had enough, He is not only going to kill the first born of the Egyptians, but also their animals AND He is going to destroy all the Egyptian Gods as well)

13) And the blood shall be to you for a token (a free pass) upon the houses where ye (you) are: and when I see the blood, I will pass over you, and the plague shall not be upon you to destroy you, when I smite (afflict) the land of Egypt.

14) And this day shall be unto you for a memorial (to remember); and ye (you) shall keep it a feast to the LORD throughout your generations; ye (you) shall keep it a feast by an ordinance (law) for ever.

15) Seven days shall ye (you) eat unleavened bread; even the first day ye (you) shall put away leaven out of your houses (now we

know where 'Passover Week' came from. By the way, that's from Palm Sunday until Easter Sunday): for whosoever eateth leavened bread frcm the first day until the seventh day, that soul shall be cut off from Israel. (what a punishment for eating leavened bread. God certainly was strict on this law)

16) And in the first day there shall be an holy convocation (a holy assembly of the people), and in the seventh day there shall be an holy convocation to you; no manner of work shall be done in them, save that which every man must eat, that only may be done of you. (the only work to be done on the days of the holy assembly of the people are that to feed each person)

17) And ye (you) shall observe the feast of unleavened bread; for in this selfsame day have I brought your armies out of the land of Egypt: therefore shall ye (you will) observe this day in your generations by an ordinance (law) for ever.

18) In the first mcnth, on the fourteenth day of the month at even (the evening of), ye (you) shall eat unleavened bread, until the one and twentieth day of the month at even (the evening of).

19) Seven days skall there be no leaven found in your houses: for whosoever eateth that which is leavened, even that soul shall be cut off from the congregation of Israel, whether he (that person) be a stranger, or born in the land.

20) Ye (you) shall eat nothing leavened (anything that makes dough rise); in al your habitations shall ye (you) eat unleavened (without yeast or any rising ingredient) bread.

21) Ther Moses called for all the elders of Israel, and said unto them (the elders of Israel), Draw out and take you a lamb according to your families, and kill the passover.

22) And ye (you) shall take a bunch of hyssop (a plant used for purification), and dip it (the hyssop) in the blood that is in the bason, and strike the lintel (the cross-member of the door frame) and the two side posts with the blood that is in the bason; and none of you shall go out at the door of his house until the morning.

23) For the LORD will pass through to smite (kill) the Egyptians; and when he (the Lord) seeth the blood upon the lintel, and on the two side posts, the LORD will pass over the door, and will

not suffer the destroyer (death angel in this particular situation) to come in unto your houses to smite (kill) you.

24) And ye (you) shall observe this thing for an ordinance (law) to thee (you) and to thy (your) sons for ever.

25) And it shall come to pass, when ye (you) be come to the land which the LORD will give you, according as he hath (the Lord has) promised, that ye (you) shall (will) keep this service.

26) And it shall come to pass, when your children shall say unto you, What mean ye by this service (why do you do this act)?

27) That ye shall (you will) say, It is the sacrifice of the LORD's passover, who passed over the houses of the children of Israel in Egypt, when he (the Lord) smote (killed) the Egyptians, and delivered our houses. And the people bowed the head and worshipped.

28) And the children of Israel went away, and did as the LORD had commanded Moses and Aaron, so did they (the children of Israel put the blood of the sacrifice on the door posts and cross-beam).

29) And it came to pass, that at midnight the LORD smote (killed) all the firstborn in the land of Egypt, from the firstborn of Pharaoh that sat on his (Pharaoh's) throne unto the firstborn of the captive that was in the dungeon; and all the firstborn of cattle. (from the highest to the lowest)

30) And Pharaoh rose up in the night, he (Pharoah), and all his (Pharaoh's) servants, and all the Egyptians; and there was a great cry (a great mourning) in Egypt; for there was not a house where there was not one dead. **(all these miracles took approximately eight years to complete from the first to the last. We expect things to be done in a few minutes or overnight. God, at times, has to take His time doing things)**

31) And he (Pharaoh) called for Moses and Aaron by night, and said, Rise up, and get you forth (leave here) from among my people, both ye (you) and the children of Israel; and go, serve the LORD, as ye (you) have said.

32) Also take your flocks and your herds, as ye (you) have said, and be gone; and bless me also. (the Israelites leaving Pharaoh and Egypt is going to be a blessing to Pharaoh just to get rid of

the Israelites)

33) And the Egyptians were urgent upon the people, that they might send them out of the land in haste; for they said, We be all dead men. (the Egyptians told the Israelites to leave, helped the Israelites pack, and made the Israelites leave Egypt)

34) And the people (Israelites) took their dough before it was leavened, their kneadingtroughs being bound up in their clothes upon their shoulders.

35) And the children of Israel did according to the word of Moses; and they (the Israelites) borrowed of the Egyptians jewels of silver, and jewels of gold, and raiment:

36) And the LORD gave the people (the Israelites) favour in the sight of the Egyptians, so that they (the Egyptians) lent unto them (let the Israelites borrow) such things as they (the Israelites) required.   And they (the Israelites) spoiled (ruined) the Egyptians.

37) And the children of Israel journeyed from Rameses to Succoth, about six hundred thousand (600,000 men plus women and children) on foot that were men, beside children.

38) And a mixed multitude went up also with them (the children of Israel); and flocks, and herds, even very much cattle.

39) And they (the Israelites) baked unleavened cakes of the dough which they (the Israelites) brought forth out of Egypt, for it (the bread) was not leavened; because they (the Israelites) were thrust out of Egypt, and could not tarry (linger), neither had they (the Israelites) prepared for themselves any victual (food).

40) Now the sojourning of the children of Israel, who dwelt in Egypt, was four hundred and thirty years. **(the children of Israel temporarily stayed in Egypt for 430 years)**

41) **And it came to pass at the end of the four hundred and thirty years (430 years), even the selfsame day it came to pass (to the day of the 430 year anniversary), that all the hosts of the LORD went out from the land of Egypt.**

42) It is a night to be much observed unto the LORD for bringing them (the Israelites) out from the land of Egypt: this is that night of the LORD to be observed of all the children of Israel in their generations (forever).

43) And the LORD said unto Moses and Aaron, This is the ordinance (law) of the passover: There shall no stranger eat thereof:

44) But every man's servant that is bought for money (slave), when thou hast circumcised him, then shall he (the servant) eat thereof.

45) A foreigner and an hired servant (hired worker) shall not eat thereof (shall not eat of the unleavened bread).

46) In one house shall it (the unleavened bread) be eaten; thou shalt not carry forth ought (you will not save) of the flesh (the sacrifice) abroad out of the house; neither shall ye (you) break a bone thereof.

47) All the congregation of Israel shall keep it (the law).

48) And when a stranger shall sojourn (temporarily stay) with thee (you), and will keep the passover to the LORD, let all his males (offspring) be circumcised, and then let him (the stranger) come near and keep it (continue to celebrate the passover); and he (the stranger) shall be as one that is born in the land (in today's terms, the stranger Crosses over to Christianity): for no uncircumcised person shall eat thereof.

49) One law shall be to him (the Israelite) that is homeborn, and unto the stranger that sojourned (that temporarily stays) among you (the Israelites).

50) Thus did all the children of Israel; as the LORD commanded Moses and Aaron, so did they. (the children of Israel did everything that the Lord commanded Moses and Aaron to do)

51) And it came to pass the selfsame day (later on that day), that the LORD did bring the children of Israel out of the land of Egypt by their armies.

Exodus 13:1-22

1) And the LORD spake unto Moses, saying,

2) Sanctify unto me all the firstborn, whatsoever (whichever one the child is, male or female) openeth (seeing the 'light of day' as Heavenly Angel Lay Lay pointed out to me, being born of water. More about this in my book MATTHEW'S WORD

'TWO':REAL WORD OF GOD BIBLE) the womb among the children of Israel, both of man and of beast: it is mine.

3) And Moses said unto the people, Remember this day, in which ye (you) came out from Egypt, out of the house of bondage (the slavery of Egypt); for by strength of hand the LORD brought you out from this place (Egypt): there shall no leavened bread be eaten.

4) This day came ye (you) out in the month Abib. (ok, here is the actual name of the first month of the first year of the new calendar)

5) And it shall be when the LORD shall bring thee (you) into the land of the Canaanites, and the Hittites, and the Amorites, and the Hivites, and the Jebusites, which he (God) sware (promised) unto thy (your) fathers to give thee (you), a land flowing with milk and honey, that thou shalt (you will) keep this service in this month. (the same day of the same month will be when the Israelites go into the land of Canaan. This tells me the amount of time the Israelites go from Egypt to Canaan will be at least one years journey)

6) Seven days thou shalt (you will) eat unleavened bread, and in the seventh day shall be a feast to the LORD.

7) Unleavened bread shall be eaten seven days; and there shall no leavened bread be seen with thee (you), neither shall there be leaven seen with thee (you) in all thy quarters (your living places or houses).

8) And thou shalt shew thy (you will show your) son in that day, saying, This is done because of that which the LORD did unto me when I came forth out of Egypt.

9) And it (the Passover) shall be for a sign unto thee (you) upon thine (your) hand, and for a memorial between thine (your) eyes, that the LORD's law may be in thy (your) mouth: for with a strong hand hath the LORD brought thee (you) out of Egypt.

10) Thou (you) shalt therefore keep this ordinance (law) in his season from year to year (this is a yearly observance).

11) And it shall be (at the appointed time) when the LORD shall bring thee (you) into the land of the Canaanites, as he (God) sware (promises) unto thee (you) and to thy (your) fathers, and

shall give it (Canaan) thee (to you),

12) That thou (you) shalt set apart unto the LORD all that openeth the matrix (the womb), and every firstling (first born) that cometh of a beast which thou hast; the males shall be the LORD's.

13) And every firstling (first born) of an ass thou shalt redeem with a lamb; and if thou wilt (you will) not redeem it, then thou shalt (you will) break his (the animal's) neck: and all the firstborn of man among thy (your) children shalt thou (will you) redeem.

14) And it shall be (at the time) when thy (your) son asketh thee (you) in time to come, saying, What is this? that thou (you) shalt (will) say unto him, By strength of hand the LORD brought us (the Israelites) out from Egypt, from the house of bondage:

15) And it came to pass (eventually), when Pharaoh would hardly let us go, that the LORD slew (killed) all the firstborn in the land of Egypt, both the firstborn of man, and the firstborn of beast: therefore I sacrifice to the LORD all that openeth the matrix (are born of the water, born of the womb), being males; but all the firstborn of my children I redeem.

16) And it shall be for a token (a remembrance) upon thine (your) hand, and for frontlets (a decorative band worn on the forehead) between thine (your) eyes: for by strength of hand the LORD brought us forth out of Egypt.

17) And it came to pass (eventually), when Pharaoh had let the people go (the Israelites), that God led them (the Israelites) not through the way of the land of the Philistines, although that was near; for God said, Lest peradventure (foresee) the people (the Israelites) repent when they (the Israelites) see war, and they (the Israelites) return to Egypt: (this blows the atheist's theory about the Israelites going through the Red Sea at the Eastern Bank where the water is very shallow, instead of in the middle of the Red Sea where God had to part the waters for the Israelites to pass through. This scripture specifically says the Israelites didn't go by way of the Philistines which was the easy way and near).

18) But God led the people about, through the way of the wilderness of the Red sea: and the children of Israel went up

harnessed (getting control) out of the land of Egypt.

19) And Moses took the bones of Joseph with him: for he (Joseph foretold of this event taking place) had straitly sworn the children of Israel, saying, God will surely visit you; and ye shall (you will) carry up my bones away hence (from Egypt) with you.

20) And they (the Israelites) took their journey from Succoth, and encamped in Etham, in the edge of the wilderness. (Succoth to Etham is about 25 miles or 41.75 kilometers which is a day's journey by camel, but with all the people walking it took longer, that's why God insisted on three days to journey into the desert)

21) And the LORD went before them (the Israelites) by day in a pillar of a cloud, to lead them the way; and by night in a pillar of fire, to give them light; to go by day and night: (the Israelites never stopped, they switched off and on taking turns pulling and driving the wagons and camels, etc.)

22) He (God) took not away the pillar of the cloud by day, nor the pillar of fire by night, from before the people.

(CONTINUED IN: HEAVENLY ANGEL LAY LAY
EXPLAINS
WHAT 'MANY ARE CALLED, BUT FEW ARE CHOSEN'
REALLY MEANS)

BIBLIOGRAPHY

1. Encarta ® World English Dictionary © & (P) 1998-2004 Microsoft Corporation. All rights reserved.

2. Merriam Webster's Collegiate Dictionary Tenth Edition (1993), United States of America.

3. The Holy Bible King James Version (1998), B. B. Kirkbride Bible Co., Inc. Indianapolis, IN..USA

www.ingramcontent.com/pod-product-compliance
Lightning Source LLC
LaVergne TN
LVHW091211080426
835509LV00006B/933